The Wild Flowers of Jersey

Deirdre A. Shirreffs

Brambleby Books

The Wild Flowers of Jersey
Copyright © Deirdre A. Shirreffs 2015

All Rights Reserved

No part of this book may be reproduced in any form by photocopying or by any electronic or mechanical means, including information, storage or retrieval systems, without permission in writing from both the copyright owner and the publisher of this book.

Deirdre A. Shirreffs has asserted her right under the Copyright, Design and Patent Act, 1988, to be identified as author of this work.

A CIP catalogue record for this book is available from the British Library

ISBN 9781908241337

Published 2015 by
Brambleby Books Ltd., UK
www.bramblebybooks.co.uk

Design and layout by Tanya Warren, creatixdesign.co.uk
Cover photo by Deirdre Shirreffs
Printed on FSC paper and bound by Cambrian Printers UK

The Wild Flowers of Jersey

This book is dedicated to the memory of my parents,
Derek and Margaret Chalmers.

Preface

This book arose from a talk I gave to the Jersey Flower Club. The talk was very well received and afterwards many of the ladies came up to me commenting how much they had learnt about plants they had known since childhood. One of the ladies suggested I turned my talk into a book and so here it is! My love of flowers started at an early age, when my mother used to take me for walks and tell me the names of the wild flowers we saw. I later studied botany at university, qualifying with an Honours degree and a Ph.D.. I have lived in Jersey for over 20 years and have come to know its flora well and it is indeed a special place for nature lovers. I hope this little book will help all those who want to know about the flowers they encounter while walking around our beautiful island.

Contents

Places to See Wild Flowers	12	Ragged Robin	38
Flower types	14	Nottingham Catchfly	38
Pollination	14	Wild Gladiolus	39
The Doctrine of Signatures	16	Jersey Orchid	39
The Names of Plants	16	The Orchid Field	40
Gorse, Furze, Whin	17	Pyramidal Orchid	41
Broom	18	Purple Loosestrife	41
Blackthorn, Sloe	18	Pendulous Sedge	42
Hawthorn, May	19	Green-winged Orchid	42
Daffodil	20	Yellow Flag	43
Winter Heliotrope	21	Gladdon	44
Snowdrop	22	Navelwort	44
Summer Snowflake	22	Herb Bennet	45
Three-cornered Leek	23	Greater Celandine	45
Lesser Celandine	23	Elder	46
Common Dog Violet	24	Honeysuckle	47
Primrose	25	Clematis	47
Greater Stitchwort	26	Foxglove	48
Spring Beauty	27	Wood Sage	49
Lords and Ladies, Wild Arum	27	Fennel	49
Pink Oxalis	28	Red Valerian	50
Enchanter's Nightshade	29	Tufted Vetch	50
Red Campion	30	Melilot	51
Sea Campion	30	Balm-leaved Figwort	51
Bluebell	31	Nipplewort	52
Butcher's Broom	32	Hedge Bindweed	52
Alexanders	33	Field Bindweed	53
Hogweed	34	Sea Bindweed	53
Wild Carrot	34	Dodder	54
Dog Rose	35	Poppy	55
Burnet Rose	36	Corn Marigold	55
Spotted Rockrose	36	Scentless Mayweed	56
Evening Primrose	37	Pineappleweed	56

Ox-eye Daisy	57	Jersey Thrift	75
Mexican Fleabane	57	Alderney Sea Lavender	75
Canadian Fleabane	58	Rock Samphire	76
Common Fleabane	58	Thyme	77
Cape Cudweed	58	Sea Radish	77
Yarrow	59	Rough Star Thistle	78
Buck's-horn Plantain	60	Carline Thistle	78
Mugwort	60	Hottentot Fig	78
Germander Speedwell	61	Mallow	79
Lady's Bedstraw	61	Salsify	80
Goosegrass, Cleavers	62	Teasel	80
Pellitory-of-the-wall	63	Scarlet Pimpernel	81
Ivy-leaved Toadflax	63	Bell Heather	82
English Stonecrop	64	Ling	82
Black Nightshade	65	Ragwort	83
Woody Nightshade, Bittersweet	65	Great Mullein	83
Thorn Apple	66	Spear Thistle	84
Kangaroo Apple	66	Tormentil	85
Lesser Burdock	67	Great Willowherb	85
Annual Mercury	68	Herb Robert	86
Quaking Grass	68	Gallant Soldier	86
Hare's Tail	69	Green Alkanet	87
Marram Grass	69	Ramping Fumitory	87
Sea Beet	70	Sheep's Bit Scabious	88
Yellow Horned Poppy	71	Heath Milkwort	88
Sea Holly	71	Water Mint	89
Tamarisk	72	Autumn Ladies' Tresses	90
Argentum	72	Blackberry, Bramble	90
Tree Lupin	73	Ivy	91
Restharrow	73	German Ivy	92
Common Centaury	74	Bibliography and Further Reading	93
Sea Kale	74	Index of Common Names	94

Introduction

Jersey is a small island, 9 by 5 miles (14.5 by 8 km), with an area of 45 square miles (116 square km), situated in the Bay of St Malo 15 miles (24 km) from the French coast. Yet amazingly about 1,500 different species of flowering plant grow in this small island – this compares well with the approximately 2400 species found in the whole of the UK and Ireland. So why do so many flowers grow in this small area? There are three main reasons.

1) Although small, Jersey has a very varied geology and topography and hence a wide variety of habitats. Indeed it has practically all those found in the UK with the exception of mountains. Thus there are woods, marshes, grasslands, cliffs, sand dunes, all contributing their own species to the total.

2) Jersey's location between the UK and mainland Europe means that it has plant species from both areas. An example of this is the plant Lords and Ladies where both the British and the mainland European species are common in Jersey.

3) Jersey's mild climate allows garden escapes to flourish and spread. In the past, gardeners were allowed to dump their waste in the countryside and many survived to colonise the island. Now laws prevent this, but garden plants still continue to escape and become naturalised, sometimes becoming pests. Russian Vine, also known as Mile-a-Minute Vine, Japanese Knotweed and Hottentot Fig are all common in the countryside, defying attempts to remove them. Pampas Grass can also be seen colonising neglected fields, spreading quickly by its wind-blown

seeds. Many of these aliens give away their origins with exotic names – Cape Cudweed, Mexican Fleabane and Canadian Fleabane to name but a few.

This book is intended to give walkers and nature lovers a guide to a hundred or so of Jersey's wild flowers, with some of their folklore and history. Trees are not included. The species are arranged in seasonal order, from spring through to winter. All the photographs were taken in Jersey. The herbal cures are mentioned for interest only and are not to be recommended!

Places to See Wild Flowers

Woodlands
Typical deciduous woodlands are found across the island. Jersey slopes down from north to south, and many of its woodlands are found in the valleys which run towards the south. Good areas to visit are Creepy Valley, St Peter's Valley, Fern Valley and St Catherine's Woods. Oak, Holm Oak, Elm and Sweet Chestnut have been growing here for centuries but are now joined by Sycamore. The ground flora of these woods is similar to that in British woods, although there are some unusual differences. Wood Anemone, Wood Sorrel and Dog's Mercury are all rare in Jersey for no apparent reason. The pine tree with long needles and huge cones is the Monterey Pine from California.

Sand Dunes
The sand dunes in St Ouen's Bay are of international importance and have been designated a Site of Special Interest (SSI). Many species grow there, including rarities, and it is well worth a visit. Sand dunes also occur at Ouaisne and Gorey.

Grasslands
The orchid field in St Ouen's Bay is a must to visit in late May and June. Other wet grasslands are found in St Peter's Valley, Fern Valley and beside St Catherine's Woods. Dry grasslands are found at Noirmont.

Cliffs
Because Jersey slopes from north to south, most of the cliffs are found on the north coast, although there are also cliffs in the south-west corner. Cliff paths make it easy for

walkers to find flowers and enjoy the spectacular views. In spring you will find woodland plants such as primroses and bluebells growing there, and in summer the dreaded Hottentot Fig flowers on the south-west cliffs.

Heathlands
There are several heathland areas in Jersey. Worth visiting are Portelet Common, Les Landes and La Lande du Ouest. These are all designated as SSIs, Sites of Special Interest.

Marshland
Both freshwater and salt marshes are found in Jersey. The name Samares means saltmarsh, although there are none there now. Look in St Ouen's Bay just behind the sea wall. Freshwater marshes are found at Ouaisne, St Ouen's Bay and Grouville.

Flower Types

Flowering plants are split into two groups, Monocotyledons and Dicotyledons. The Monocotyledons typically have long narrow leaves and their flower parts are in multiples of three. They include Daffodils, Bluebells, Snowdrops, Grasses and Orchids. The Dicotyledons typically have broader leaves and flower parts in four or five. They include Primroses, daisies, vetches and violets. The Daisy family have unusual flowers known as Composites. What appears to be one flower is actually a head of many small flowers or florets. These can be tubular, as in the yellow centre of a Daisy, or strap shaped, as in its white outer layer. Dandelions look fluffy because they are entirely made from strap-shaped florets. Another family of Dicotyledons is the Umbellifers where the flowers are in large flat-topped 'umbels', each with many small flowers. These provide more visual impact to attract the pollinating insects.

Pollination

Flowering plants are pollinated in two main ways – by wind or insect. Wind-pollinated plants do not require showy flowers to attract insects and their small flowers often go unnoticed. Grasses and many of our deciduous trees fall into this group. Oak, Sycamore, Beech and Hazel are examples, all having separate male and female catkins. Because wind pollination is a chancy business the flowers have to produce copious amounts of pollen, much to the discomfort of hay fever sufferers.

Insect-pollinated plants have many adaptations to attract their insect visitors. Large, bright-coloured petals signal to the insects that there may be a nectar reward. Some petals have marks known as honey guides to point the way to the nectar. Remember that insect vision is different from ours and even a seemingly monochrome flower may have guides which the insect can see using their ultraviolet vision. Some plants are very adapted to their insect pollinators – Honeysuckle has a long tube which only a moth's long tongue can reach and its scent is released mostly at night to attract the moths. The Bee Orchid has evolved to resemble its pollinating insect which then attempts to mate with it, getting covered in pollen as it does so!

Have you ever noticed that many of our early spring flowers are white or yellow? Lesser Celandine, Primrose and Wood Anemone are examples. Research showed that these flowers were at a higher temperature than the surrounding air and so attracted the few insects around at that time of year. The colours of late spring are pink and blue, as demonstrated by the Bluebells and Red Campion. Bees cannot see red and so very few of our wild flowers are red and those only flower in summer when insects are at their most abundant – Poppies for example.

The most complicated pollination mechanism of our native plants must be that of Lords and Ladies. Its flower consists of a hood-like spathe with a club-shaped spadix in the centre. This emits a smell of rotting carrion and is also hotter than the surrounding air so that small flies are attracted to it. They crawl down the spadix or slip down the slippery spathe into the bottom chamber only to find themselves trapped by a ring of hairs. In the chamber the male flowers are above the female flowers. The flies remain trapped until the male flowers ripen and shed their pollen over them. The ring of hairs then withers and allows the pollen-covered flies to escape and fly to another plant where they get trapped all over again and their pollen load can fertilise that plant's female flowers.

The Doctrine of Signatures

In the Middle Ages people believed that God had created a plant to cure every disease and He had designed them to resemble the disease they could cure; this was known as the Doctrine of Signatures. Many of these plants were given names ending in 'wort'. Thus the spotted leaves of Lungwort were thought to show that it could be used to cure tuberculosis, and the tri-lobed leaves of Liverwort, resembling the three-lobed liver, could cure diseases of that organ.

The Names of Plants

As well as the common names of the flowers, I have also given the scientific Latin names in brackets. Common names can be ambiguous – the same plant can have several common names and the same name can apply to several plants. Jersey has its own language, a form of Jersey Norman French known as Jerriais, and many of the plants have Jersey French names which I have also given.

Gorse, Furze, Whin
(*Ulex europaeus*) du geon

An old country saying states that "Kissing is out of fashion when the Gorse is not in bloom", but lovers have no need to worry as Gorse flowers all year round. However, the main flowering period is in spring when the heaths and commons have a magnificent display of golden yellow flowers. These smell of coconut and are followed by seed pods resembling miniature furry pea pods. These dry out and explode with an audible pop on hot summer days, scattering the seeds.

It burns well (too well, which explains why heath fires spread so rapidly), and in the past it was used as fuel. Jersey homes sometimes had a furze oven which supposedly gave the food a special flavour. It was also used for animal fodder.

It is an important plant for the rare Dartford Warbler which nests in it and sings from its top branches.

A related species, the Western Gorse also grows on the heaths in Jersey. It is low-growing and, unlike its larger relative, it only flowers once a year – in late summer. Its flowers are a darker golden yellow.

Broom
(*Cytisus scoparius*)   **du genet**

This is closely related to Gorse with similar flowers but without the prickly stems. The French and Jersey-French name is 'genet', hence the Route des Genets in St Brelade, although no Broom grows there now. Broom also gave its name to the Plantagenet kings of England as their followers wore a sprig of Broom to identify themselves in battle – the name Plantagenet coming from 'planta genista'. The stems of Broom can be manipulated into curves and so are very useful to flower arrangers. In the past they were tied together and made into brooms. Despite the yellow colour of the flowers they make a green dye. The flower buds can be eaten or added to salads, and the flowers can be used to make a nice wine. A subspecies, Prostrate Broom, grows on the Western cliffs, with flattened silvery stems which grow close to the ground. The silvery look is due to many small hairs.

Blackthorn, Sloe
(*Prunus spinosa*)   **d'la nethe epingne, eune prunelle**

This is one of the first shrubs to flower in spring, the white flowers appearing before the leaves. The flowers

are followed by blue-black sloes in autumn. These are a kind of wild plum, but they are far too bitter to eat, although they can be used to make sloe gin. It is possible that the Blackthorn is a parent of the domestic plum. The Blackthorns in Jersey have fewer thorns than those in the UK.

The wood is very hard and is traditionally used for making shillelaghs.

Hawthorn, May
(*Crataegus monogyna*)　　　　　d'la blanche epingne

Hawthorn is a Jersey native which has been used for hedging for centuries. The flowers appear after the leaves, unlike the similar Blackthorn. The red haws which ripen in autumn are enjoyed by birds. 'Haw' comes from the Anglo-Saxon word for hedge.

It is unlucky to take the blossom into the house – one suggestion to explain this is that the sickly sweet smell of the blossom reminded people of the smell of death in an

age when bodies were laid out in the front parlour. A Scottish saying tells you to "Cast not a clout till May be out", meaning to keep your winter clothes on until the hawthorn flowers.

If you were ever puzzled by the nursery rhyme about gathering nuts in May, it actually refers to "nuts of May" where the nuts are the buds of the May tree.

Daffodil
(*Narcissus pseudonarcissus*)
des g'zettes

Many of the Daffodils growing along the roadsides are escapes from gardens and flower fields. These will gradually revert to the wild type. However, true wild Daffodils do occur in Jersey, making a beautiful display

in the woods, such as Noirmont Woods, and also growing on the cliffs. They are paler and more delicate than garden Daffodils, with drooping flowers. Unlike garden Daffodils, they spread by seed to cover the woodland floor. It is also known as the Lent Lily because of its flowering time.

Winter Heliotrope
(*Petasites fragrans*)   du pas d'ane

This is sometimes called Coltsfoot in Jersey. The real Coltsfoot (*Tussilago farfara*) is a close relative which is common in the UK but rare in Jersey. Unlike the real Coltsfoot which flowers before the leaves appear, Winter Heliotrope produces its leaves and flowers at the same time. The pinkish flowers are vanilla scented. The leaves have been used to make a herbal tobacco. Although well-naturalised, it is a garden escape.

Snowdrop
(*Galanthus nivalis*)
des bouonnefemmes

A garden escape which has become naturalised in shady areas. It was growing in England by the time of Elizabeth I. Its beautiful white flowers are one of the delights of spring, appearing from January onwards. In the past girls collected bunches on Candlemas Day (2nd February) to decorate the church, giving it the name Candlemas Bells. Another old name is Fair Maids of February. The six white petals are arranged in two whorls of three, the inner ring forming a bell in the centre with green markings, the outer three spreading out and pure white. Nivalis is the Latin for snow.

Summer Snowflake
(*Leucojum aestivum*)

Despite the name, this is a spring-flowering plant. It is native to Britain, growing on the banks of the River

Loddon, a tributary of the Thames, hence its other name of Loddon Lily. In Jersey it is a garden escape which has become naturalised in woods and on roadsides. The flowers are like wide, white bells with green edges. Unlike Snowdrops, all six petals form the bell.

Three-cornered Leek
(*Allium triquetrum*)
d'l'as sauvage

This pretty flower resembles a white bluebell, but people who pick it soon realise their mistake as it smells strongly of onions. The stem is triangular in section, hence the name. Although it is now common along the hedgerows and roadsides, it was originally grown in gardens and is native to the Western Mediterranean.

Lesser Celandine
(*Ficaria verna*)
du morrhouiton

This pretty little plant is one of the earliest spring flowers, growing in woods and shady places. A close relative of buttercups, its yellow flowers can have anything from seven to twelve petals. The leaves

are dark green and often blotched with lighter or darker patches. The little bulbils at ground level were thought to resemble piles, hence the old name of Pilewort. The young leaves were eaten to cure scurvy, and a juice from the roots was used to cure warts. The name Celandine is thought

to come from the Greek word for swallow as the plant was supposed to flower when the swallows arrived. William Wordsworth was a great lover of the Lesser Celandine and wrote two poems to it – yet the carver of his gravestone mistakenly pictured the Greater Celandine which is very different and not related!

Common Dog Violet
(*Viola riviniana*)   **du coucou**

This violet is common all over the island in woods and on roadside verges. The 'dog' of the name means it is unimportant as its flowers are unscented. In late spring

cleistogamous flowers are produced – these never open yet produce seeds asexually. Violet seeds are quite large and have an attached oil body – this is attractive to ants who carry the seeds away and so disperse them. Violets are known as shy because the flowers tend to hide amongst the leaves. The Sweet Violet has a beautiful scent which is elusive. This is because the perfume contains a chemical which prevents your nose from smelling it again for a time.

Primrose
(*Primula vulgaris*)　　　　　　　　　**des pip'soles**

The name Primrose literally means first rose, from the Latin *'prima rosa'*. Primroses are common in Jersey, although they tend to be absent from roadside banks. Often they are naturalised in graveyards and you can also find them in many of the island's woods. The flowers are borne singly, pale yellow with a darker 'eye'. There are two kinds of flower, one has the stigma at the top of the flower tube (looking like a pin) and one has the ring of stamens at the top of the tube (these look like the 'thrums' or loose threads at the edge of woven cloth). The separation of the flowers into these pin and thrum types ensures cross-pollination. In the past an ointment made from Primroses was used to rid faces of freckles or suntans and an infusion was used to treat coughs. Primrose tea was drunk to cure rheumatism and to aid insomnia. It was considered unlucky to bring a single

flower into the house, and in some areas it was unlucky to bring in fewer than thirteen flowers. Children who ate the flowers were supposed to be able to see fairies.

Primroses were the favourite flower of Benjamin Disraeli and in 1882 Primrose Day was created. It is on the 19th April, the day of his death (in 1881), and each year primroses were laid by his statue in Parliament Square.

Greater Stitchwort
(*Stellaria holostea*)

This pretty spring flower grows in woodland and on shady banks. It is common in Jersey but absent from the other Channel Islands. The stems are thin and weak and the plant uses other plants for support. It is closely related to the much smaller flowered Chickweed. It was regarded as a thunder flower and picking it would supposedly cause a thunderstorm – White Campion was similar. As its name suggests, it was used to treat a stitch in the side, and also to mend broken bones. If a woman ate it she would have a son. Another name is Star of Bethlehem.

Spring Beauty
(*Claytonia perfoliata*)

This plant is unusual as the small white flowers grow out of the centre of the fleshy leaves – the Latin *perfoliata* meaning 'through the leaf'. The leaves can be used in salads, and indeed some local restaurants collect them for their dishes. It was introduced into Britain in the early 19th century and was first recorded in Jersey in 1908. Another name for it is Miners' Lettuce because Miner's in the American Gold Rush ate it to prevent getting scurvy – a disease caused by lack of vitamin C.

Lords and Ladies, Wild Arum
(*Arum italicum* **and** *maculatum*)
du pitouais

Lords and Ladies is possibly the plant with the most English names – over one hundred have been listed, many referring to the phallic appearance

of the curious flower. Two species grow in Jersey – the Common Lords and Ladies which can have spotted leaves, although spotted leaves are less common in Jersey than in Britain where it is a common hedgerow plant, and the Southern or Italian Lords and Ladies which is common in mainland Europe and often has white veins on its leaves. The leaves of the Italian Lords and Ladies appear in the autumn, whereas those of the Common Lords and Ladies do not grow until the spring. All parts of these plants are poisonous, especially the spike of red berries which appears in autumn and Wild Arum causes most of the poisoning cases seen in Accident and Emergency departments in the UK. However, in Tudor times, the starch from the underground tubers of the Common Lords and Ladies was used to starch the ruffs that noble men and women wore around their necks, causing terrible blisters on the hands of the poor laundresses!

Pink Oxalis
(*Oxalis debilis*)   du trefl'yea ouognons

This pretty pink flower with clover-like leaves is common along the roadsides. It is native to South America and spreads rapidly by means of little bulbils at the base of the stem. Another Pink Oxalis from South America is a common garden escape and lacks the bulbils, so does not become a pest. Both are related to the delicate white Wood Sorrel which is common in British woods, although rare in Jersey. About ten *Oxalis* species grow in Jersey and many are troublesome weeds as they are very resistant to weedkiller.

Enchanter's Nightshade
(*Circaea lutetiana*)

This woodland plant is often an indicator of ancient woodland, although it also grows in other shady places and can be found in the wooded sections of the Railway Walk. It is related to the willowherbs. The small white flowers are followed by hooked fruits which are dispersed by passing animals. It spreads by long, creeping rhizomes and becomes a persistent weed if grown in gardens. The enchanter of the name is Circe, hence the Latin name.

Red Campion
(*Silene dioica*)
d's iliets d'fosse

This is a very common species, found in woods and roadsides. It flowers from April to September, but in Jersey's mild climate you are likely to find some in flower all year round. As its Latin name suggests it is dioecious, meaning that the male and female flowers are on separate plants.

It is closely related to White Campion and often hybridises with it. Any plant with pale pink flowers is likely to be a hybrid. White Campion produces its scent at night to attract the night-flying moths which pollinate it. Red Campion is a perennial plant, but White Campion is usually an annual, although it can be a short-lived perennial.

Sea Campion
(*Silene uniflora*)
d's iliets d'rotchi

The Sea Campion grows around the coast as its name suggests, but it is

also found inland. It grows in low dense mats and has lovely white flowers with an inflated calyx. It is closely related to the Bladder Campion which also occurs in Jersey, although it is rare. At one time they were thought to be variants of the same species.

Bluebell
(*Hyacinthoides non-scripta*)   des clioches de Careme

A Bluebell wood in spring is a beautiful sight. The native Bluebell, also known as the English Bluebell, is common in Jersey growing in woods such as Fern Valley, but also growing on the heaths and cliffs where bracken often

gives it the shelter from the summer heat that the trees give the woodland plants. The plants are sensitive to trampling as this kills the leaves and prevents them from making food to replenish the bulb for the next year. In Tudor times the bulbs were used to make a glue, and the starch in them was used to starch the ruffs.

The Spanish Bluebell, a garden escape, now also grows wild in Jersey and is becoming a problem as it is invasive. It also hybridises with the native Bluebell which is in danger of becoming lost. The native Bluebell is more delicate in appearance, with a curving flower stalk from which the 'bells' hang down on one side. The petals are recurved, curving back to touch the bell.

Butcher's Broom
(*Ruscus aculeatus*)
du fregon

This is a small woodland shrub, found in Creepy Valley, St Peter's Valley and St Catherine's Woods, among others. The name comes from the time when

butchers used its spiny branches to scrub their wooden chopping tables. An alternative name is Knee Holly which is self-explanatory! It is the only British member of the lily family which is woody. The spiky 'leaves' are actually flattened stems. The tiny white flowers which grow out from the middle of these 'leaves' are either male or female, each sex being on a different plant. The female flowers ripen into bright red berries in autumn.

Alexanders
(*Smyrnium olusatrum*) d'l'alisandre

An easily recognised umbellifer with its dark green leaves and yellow green flowers. The flowers appear in the spring. It is common all over the island. Another Jersey-

French name means wild celery, so it may originally have been a garden plant in Jersey. It originates from Southern Europe and was widely grown as a pot herb. The stems and roots can be boiled and the flower heads used in salads. The name is a shortened form of the Mediaeval name, Parsley of Alexandria. This may refer to its place of origin or may mean that Alexander the Great discovered it.

Hogweed
(*Heracleum sphondylium*)   **d'la benarde**

A very common white umbellifer. The name Hogweed refers to the fact that it was used as pig fodder in the past. Boys used to make its hollow stems into pea shooters. Red Soldier Beetles are often seen on its flower heads.

Wild Carrot
(*Daucus carota*)   **d'la carotte sauvage**

The Wild Carrot has thick roots and is the ancestor of the garden carrot. It is distinguished from all other umbellifers by sometimes having one purple or red flower in the centre of the umbel. After flowering, the outer branches of the flower head curve over the rest to make a kind of

'nest' enclosing the fruits. The leaves are very feathery and smell of carrots when crushed. Very common on roadsides and field edges.

Dog Rose
(*Rosa canina*)

d'la rose sauvage

The 'dog' of the name probably refers to a common, unimportant rose when compared to the garden species, although it may also come from the fact that it was used to cure dog bites. The red hips which follow the flowers are very rich in vitamin C, containing eight times as much as oranges. They have been used since Neolithic times. Wild roses are not common in Jersey and some may have been planted in the 19th century to support the Rose political party.

Burnet Rose
(*Rosa spinosissima*)

d'la rose a sablion

This is common on the sand dunes of St Ouen's Bay, often carpeting the ground. The scented flowers are usually creamy white but some have a pink tinge. They develop into purple-black hips, the only wild rose to have hips of this colour. Burnet means 'brown' which comes from the colour of the hips before they are fully mature. The stems are very prickly. It is rare in the south of Britain and so is sometimes called the Scotch Rose.

Spotted Rock Rose
(*Tuberaria guttata*)

The Spotted Rock Rose is quite a rare plant but grows in several localities in Jersey, preferring dry soils. It flowers in June and July. The pale yellow petals each have a purple-brown spot at their base. Each flower only lasts one

day with the petals falling by afternoon. It is an annual plant and is rare in Britain. Despite its name it is not a member of the rose family.

Evening Primrose (*Oenothera* spp.) des roses d'un jour

The flowers of Evening Primroses open at night to attract the moths which pollinate them. The flowers are unusual as they change colour as they close, the yellow flower turning orange. Both the Large-flowered (*Oenothera glazioviana*) and Fragrant Evening Primroses (*Oenothera stricta*) grow in Jersey. Look for them on the dunes in St Ouen's Bay. Evening Primrose seeds are rich in oil, which is sometimes taken by menopausal women. They are related to the willowherbs as shown by the fact that both have four-petalled flowers.

Ragged Robin
(*Silene flos-cuculi*) 　　　　　　　　du coucou d'pre

A relative of Red Campion but with very divided pink petals giving it a ragged appearance. It prefers damp ground and can be found in the orchid field at St Ouen as well as other sites.

Nottingham Catchfly
(*Silene nutans*)

Catchflies are so called because they are covered in sticky hairs. This Catchfly gets its name because an early record of it was growing on the walls of Nottingham Castle. It

has nodding white or pinkish flowers whose petals unroll at dusk and are scented to attract moths. In Jersey it is mostly found in the west, although it also grows in a few northern sites.

Wild Gladiolus
(*Gladiolus communis*)
d's l'echelle de Jacob
Also known in Jersey as Jacks, probably linked to the Jersey-French name which translates as Jacob's Ladder. Although an escape from cultivation, it can be found in many places across Jersey. The tall spikes of dark-red flowers are very striking.

Jersey Orchid
(*Anacamptis laxiflora*)
des pentecotes
This orchid is one of Jersey's special flowers and makes a wonderful sight in the orchid field in St Ouen in late May and June. The purple flowers are well spread on the stem, hence the Latin name and the alternative name of Loose Flowered Orchid. It is not exclusive to Jersey being found in mainland Europe

and also in Guernsey. In fact, it is more common in Guernsey, but Jersey botanists named it first – apparently the Guernsey botanists were a bit annoyed!

The Orchid Field

The orchid field, properly known as Le Noir Pré, is owned and managed by the National Trust for Jersey. As well as the Jersey Orchid, several other orchid species grow there. These are the Southern Marsh Orchid (*Dactylorhiza praetermissa*), Common Spotted Orchid (*Dactylorhiza fuchsii*), and Heath Spotted Orchids (*Dactylorhiza maculata*). The last two species are quite similar and variable and also hybridise, which complicates the picture. The Common Spotted Orchid tends to have pink flowers, varying from light to dark, and elongated spots on the leaves, whereas the Heath Spotted Orchid tends to have pale purple flowers and the leaf spots are round. These four orchids are at their best in May and June, and another orchid, the Pyramidal Orchid, flowers in the field later. The field is also home to many other wild flowers, including Ragged Robin, Yellow Flag, Yellow Bartsia and Purple Loosestrife.

Pyramidal Orchid
(*Anacamptis pyramidalis*)
Easily recognised by its pyramidal spike of pink flowers. The flowers have a foxy scent and produce copious nectar for their pollinating insects.

Purple Loosestrife
(*Lythrum salicaria*)
The tall spikes of purple flowers are very attractive to bees. There are three kinds of flower, each with different anther/stigma combinations. This ensures cross-pollination. One plant can produce 3 million seeds. *Lythrum* is derived from the Greek word for 'gore' as it was used to staunch bleeding. The juice is rich in tannin and in the past was used to tan leather. They grow in damp meadows such as the orchid field in St Ouen.

Pendulous Sedge
(*Carex pendula*)
This large sedge is found growing in the damp areas of St Catherine's Wood. It gets its name from the hanging flower spikes. The seeds can be collected and sown in gardens to make an impressive specimen plant. Like all sedges it has a triangular stem.

Green-winged Orchid
(*Anacamptis morio*)
This spring-flowering orchid is common in Jersey, growing on sand dunes and established turf, such as the golf course at La Moye and neglected lawns. The 'green wing' refers to the dark green vein on the sepals. Its leaves are unspotted which distinguishes it from its close relative – the Early Purple Orchid. This also grows in Jersey but is

less common. It is referred to by Shakespeare in Ophelia's speech in Hamlet as Long Purples or Dead Man's Fingers. Also known as Gethsemane because it was thought that it grew beneath the cross at the Crucifixion and the splotches were supposed to be Christ's blood.

The name 'orchid' comes from the Greek word for testicle, as some orchids have two tubers at the base of the stem. Because of this, orchids were thought to have aphrodisiac properties.

Yellow Flag, Yellow Iris
(*Iris pseudacorus*)
du bliajeu

This yellow iris flowers in spring in wet places. You will find it in the orchid field in St Ouen's Bay or forming a yellow ribbon along the stream in St Peter's Valley. This is the flower which inspired the fleur-de-lis of France. Fleur-de-lis may be a

corruption of fleur-de-Louis. The three petals stood for faith, wisdom and valour. The flag part of the name comes from 'flagge', an old word for sword and refers to the long pointed leaves. The roots yield a black ink, whilst the seeds can be roasted and used as a coffee substitute.

Gladdon
(*Iris foetidissima*)

This woodland plant is also known as the Stinking Iris or Roast Beef Plant. If you smell some crushed leaves you will see why – they have a distinct smell of beef. Rabbits will not eat them and will starve rather than feed on them. The flowers are not very impressive, a typical iris flower but rather weedy looking. They are usually pale purple but can be yellow. The seed pod splits open in autumn to reveal a spectacular cluster of orange-red berries, much loved by flower arrangers.

Navelwort
(*Umbilicus rupestris*)
des cratchillons

Often called Pennywort because of its round fleshy leaves. This is a common plant in Jersey, growing on roadside banks and on walls. The creamy flowers grow in a spike which can be over 30cm tall. Old herbals recommended

Navelwort for burns and scalds. The juice was said to be soothing and was used to treat chilblains and inflammations. The fleshy leaves were also used as corn plasters.

Herb Bennet
(*Geum urbanum*)   d'l' herbe b'net

Also known as Wood Avens, this plant with small yellow flowers is common in woods and shady places. The name Bennet is probably after St Benedict, the founder of the Benedictine Order. The spicy smell of the roots is said to repel evil. The five petals were linked to the five wounds of Christ and so it was often depicted in church carvings. The hooked fruits catch onto passing animals which then

disperse the seeds. The name 'avens' may come from the Anglo-Saxon word for hook. Herb Bennet can be used for several ailments including upset stomach, wind and bites.

Greater Celandine
(*Chelidonium majus*)
d'l'herbe a vethues

This is not a relative of the spring-flowering Lesser Celandine but rather is related to the poppies. The flowers have four yellow petals. A poisonous bright orange juice leaks from the

cut stem and is reputed to cure warts. The Jersey-French name actually means 'herb for warts'. It is widespread in Jersey.

Elder
(*Sambucus nigra*)
du seu
Often grows near rabbit burrows or where houses once stood because it likes the nitrogen-rich soil found in these places. The creamy-white flowers grow in large flat heads where the central buds open first. They are followed by clusters of purple-black berries which hang down when ripe. They are very rich in vitamin C but unripe ones will make you ill. The berries contain the chemical sambucol which is thought to be useful against colds and flu. The name Elder comes from the Anglo Saxon for fire as the hollow branches were blown through to encourage fires to start. Young boys used to hollow the central pith from the branches to make whistles. The smell of

the flowers is said to be narcotic, and country lore tells that someone who falls asleep under an Elder tree will never again awake. The dried flowers are a good insect repellent. Yellow lichen often grows on the branches as does the Jelly Ear fungus.

Honeysuckle
(*Lonicera periclymenum*)
du chuchet

The Honeysuckle is also known as Woodbine or Eglantine. It is a relative of the elder. The flowers have a beautiful scent which is strongest in the evening to attract the night-flying moths whose long tongues can reach down the tube to feed on the nectar. The nectar is copious and can half fill the flower tube. Experiments have shown that moths can detect the smell from up to a quarter of a mile away (0.4 km). The flowers are followed by poisonous red berries. The woody stems coil clockwise round branches and can be so tight that they distort them into spirals. Its clinging habit and paired leaves gave it romantic associations and so it became a plant for lovers. Bringing Honeysuckle into the house was thought to lead to a wedding. In England the rare woodland Dormouse strips the bark to make its nests.

Clematis
(*Clematis vitalba*)   **d'la barbe d'vier bouonhomme**

Also known as Traveller's Joy and Old Man's Beard from the fluffy seed heads. This climbing plant is the closest we get to a tropical liana as it covers hedges and bushes

with a thick layer of branches. It is related to buttercups and like them has many stamens and fruits per flower. It used to be rare in Jersey but is widespread now. Look for it along the Railway Walk among other places.

Foxglove
(*Digitalis purpurea*)
de l'ouothelle de brebis

The Foxglove flowers in summer in woods and on roadside banks, its tall spikes of pink or occasionally white flowers forming spectacular displays. It is a biennial plant, forming

a rosette of large, downy leaves in the first year with the flowering spike only appearing in the second year. The name may be a corruption of 'Folksglove', i.e. referring to the fairy folk and not foxes at all.

The plant is very poisonous, containing the glycoside digitalin which is now used in heart medicines.

Wood Sage
(*Teucrium scorodonia*)
d'l'ambraise
This looks very much like Garden Sage and also has aromatic leaves. It is not a true sage, but both it and the true sages belong to the mint family. In the past the leaves were used in infusions to make a herbal tonic. In Jersey they were used in brewing and the plant was called Ambroise. It can tolerate shade well, so is a common woodland plant.

Fennel
(*Foeniculum vulgare*) **du fanon**
Fennel is an umbellifer which refers to the large flat head of flowers, known botanically as an umbel. Fennel is easily

recognised by its yellow flowers and feathery leaves which smell of aniseed. Wild Fennel does not produce a 'bulb' at the base of the stem like cultivated Fennel, but you can still use the leaves in cooking. They go particularly well with fish.

Red Valerian
(*Centranthus ruber*) du lilas d'Espagne

Originally a garden escape, Red Valerian is now common on walls across the island. It originates from the Mediterranean area but has been in Britain for centuries. Bees and butterflies love its nectar-rich flowers.

Tufted Vetch
(*Vicia cracca*)
du vechon

This spectacular vetch has one-sided spikes of purple flowers, with up to 40 flowers in each spike. It is a perennial and scrambles through the hedgerows using its tendrils.

Melilot
(*Melilotus indica*)   **du melilot**

Another member of the pea family, Melilot has spikes of yellow flowers. The plants often smell of new-mown hay because the leaves contain coumarin, the chemical which gives hay its scent. The scent intensifies on drying. Bees love the flowers for their nectar. In the past it was used to make a poultice for wounds.

Balm-leaved Figwort
(*Scrophularia scorodonia*)   **d'l'orvale**

The 'wort' part of the name tells us that it was thought to resemble figs and so be a cure for them. But what were figs? This was an old name for piles which the small, red-brown flowers were supposed to look like. Another name was Cut Finger or Carpenter Square due to the square

stem which was thought to show it could be used on wounds, such as those a careless carpenter might get. Balm-leaved Figwort is a common weed of road sides and waste ground in Jersey, although it is rare in Britain where it is replaced by Common Figwort (*Scrophularia nodosa*). Its flowers are loved by wasps which pollinate them, although the smell is unpleasant to humans.

Nipplewort
(*Lapsana communis*)
Another plant whose name refers to the Doctrine of Signatures. The closed buds were thought to resemble nipples and so were used to treat breast ulcers.

Hedge Bindweed
(*Calystegia sepium*) **des veil'yes**
This scrambles over walls and bushes, coiling anti-clockwise as it grows. The large white trumpet-shaped flowers are used by children in their games and as hats for dolls.

Field Bindweed
(*Convolvulus arvensis*) **des veil'yes de r'lie**
Field Bindweed has pretty pink flowers, much smaller than the Hedge Bindweed. It is a very common perennial, and its extensive root system growing over 2 metres deep makes it difficult to eradicate and is a pest for farmers. The growing stem tip can circle round its support in under two hours.

Sea Bindweed
(*Calystegia soldanella*) **des veil'yes de sablion**
Sea Bindweed is similar to Field Bindweed, although it is not a pest. As its name suggests, it is found near the sea,

usually in sandy areas. It grows along the ground rather than climbing. It has pink flowers with white stripes and kidney-shaped leaves.

Dodder
(*Cuscuta europaea*)   **d'la touothelle**
Dodder is related to Bindweed. It is a parasite which must gain its nutrients from a host plant – often Gorse. In summer you will often find Gorse bushes covered in a tangle of the red stems of Dodder. The stems are red because they do not contain the green pigment chlorophyll that most plants use and the leaves are reduced to small red scales along the stem. In late summer clusters of tiny pink flowers appear on the stems.

In spring the seeds germinate and the seedling stems rotate until they find a host plant to latch on to. Suckers attach the Dodder to the host plant.

The weak red stems give us the word 'doddery', meaning frail.

Poppy
(*Papaver* **spp.**) **des roses a tchian**

Poppies have long been a symbol of fertility and, since World War I, sacrifice. They have two sepals, which fall off when the flower opens, and four petals. The seedpod has holes around the top so that the seeds, and there are up to 50,000 of them per plant, are shaken out by the wind. Poppy seeds are viable in the soil for up to a century. There are two common red poppies in Jersey. The Common Poppy has a black blotch to its petals and a rounded seed capsule. It reached Britain from the Near East soon after the end of the last Ice Age. The Long-headed Poppy has petals which lack the basal black blotch and its seed capsule is elongated.

Corn Marigold
(*Glebionis segetum*)
du meneleu

The attractive flowers of the Corn Marigold make a splash of yellow at the edges of cornfields. Like all cornfield plants, they are much less common now than previously due to the use of weed-killer. Another factor in their decline is the fact that they dislike alkaline soils and the States of Jersey gave farmers a lime subsidy to 'improve' their soils.

Scentless Mayweed
(*Tripleurospermum inodorum*)   d'la m'souque

A close relative of the previous species, the Scentless Mayweed is also a weed of arable fields with white daisy-like flowers and finely cut, feathery leaves. The 'May' in the name has nothing to do with the month, but refers to a maiden instead, the plant once being used to treat female complaints.

Pineappleweed
(*Matricaria discoidea*)
As its name suggests, Pineappleweed is strongly scented, although you need a bit of imagination to recognise a

pineapple scent. It is a composite with green flowers which are rayless and so look like little green domes. It originally came from North America in the late 1800s but escaped from Kew Gardens and is now a common agricultural weed growing especially well in trampled areas such as tracks and paths. If you crush the leaves and rub them into your skin they will act as an insect repellent. Native Americans used it to line babies' cradles for this reason.

Ox-eye Daisy
(*Leucanthemum vulgare*)
d's iers de boeu
Other names for this large white daisy are Moon Daisy, Dog Daisy and Marguerite. It is common on roadsides and grasslands, and also grows on the cliffs. Juice from the stems was once used to cure sore eyes.

Mexican Fleabane
(*Erigeron karvinskianus*)
des mergots a pouochins
This pretty little pink and white daisy is originally from Mexico as its name suggests. It escaped from

gardens and now grows on almost every wall across the island. It also grows in Guernsey where it is called the St Peter Port Daisy.

Canadian Fleabane
(*Conyza canadensis*)
This was introduced around 1690 and is a common weed across the island, growing in the fields and by the roads. Its leafy stems grow up to 1.5 metres high and its small flowers appear in late summer and autumn, looking like miniature Groundsel flowers. In the UK its feathery seeds originally spread rapidly in the wind created by trains and more recently by cars on motorways.

Common Fleabane
(*Pulicaria dysenterica*)
Common Fleabane grows in damp grasslands, its yellow flowers resembling a yellow daisy with short petals. As the name suggests it was supposed to drive away fleas when burnt.

Cape Cudweed
(*Gnaphalium undulatum*)
This large Cudweed is the commonest cudweed in Jersey, growing up to 50 cm tall. As its name suggests, it is a native of South Africa. It grows on wasteland and roadsides, quickly colonising bare soil as was shown when

Holm Oak trees were cleared from an area at Noirmont – the area was soon knee deep in the silvery grey plants.

Yarrow
(*Achillea millefolium*) d'la tcherpentchiethe

Also known as Milfoil because of its finely divided leaves, this plant has many common names. It is related to the garden plant *Achillea*. Flowering in summer and autumn, the flowers are usually white, but pink forms are found.

The name Yarrow comes from the Anglo-Saxon for healer and it had many medicinal uses in the past – including as a cure for depression and colds. It was also used to staunch bleeding, hence the Jersey-French name which means Carpenter's Herb. The Greek warrior Achilles was supposed to use Yarrow to treat the wounds of his soldiers, resulting in its Latin name. Yarrow tea was drunk for colds and rheumatism. It also has insecticidal properties and is a good companion plant in the garden to keep insect pests away. A bunch of dried Yarrow hung in your wardrobe will repel moths. A yellow dye can be obtained from the leaves.

Buck's-horn Plantain
(*Plantago coronopus*)
d'la cone de cher

Several plantains grow in Jersey. The Buck's-horn Plantain is easily recognised by its divided leaves which supposedly resemble deer horns. It is the only British plantain with divided leaves. It is most common near the sea but you can also find it inland, often on dry tracks where the conditions resemble those near the sea. The leaves grow in a rosette with the flowering stems emerging from the centre. The leaves and flower stems are unusual in that they spread out horizontally first and only turn upwards at the ends. Like other plantains they are wind-pollinated. In the past it was thought to cure a bite from a mad dog.

Mugwort
(*Artemisia vulgaris*) **d'l'herbe de St Jean**

A member of the daisy family, its leaves have silvery undersides. They are aromatic and were laid in clothes

as an insect repellent. They were also used instead of hops to flavour beer. Botanist Nicholas Culpeper (1616-54) recommended Mugwort for 'female disorders'. It is common on field edges, roadsides and waste places.

Germander Speedwell
(*Veronica chamaedrys*)
du terretre

The Latin name means 'true icon' and refers to St Veronica who used her handkerchief to wipe Christ's face on the way to Calgary and found his image was left on the cloth. The petals are a bright blue but fall soon after the flower is picked – perhaps explaining the speedwell part of the name. The Germander part of the name comes from the Greek word for ground oak because its leaves are supposed to resemble the leaves of that plant. The flowers were used to relieve sore eyes. A common grassland plant.

Lady's Bedstraw
(*Galium verum*)
du myi d'mielle

The Lady of the name is the Virgin Mary, and legend states that she lay on a bed of this plant at the Nativity. Because of this it was thought to help women in childbirth, so was used to stuff mattresses, hence

the bedstraw part of the name. The flowers smell of new-mown hay because they contain the chemical coumarin. The froth of yellow flowers makes it easily recognisable, growing on roadsides and field edges. It was used to curdle milk for cheese-making. It is also the main food plant of the spectacular Elephant Hawk Moth. Hedge Bedstraw, a close relative, is very similar and grows in similar places but has white flowers. It is more common than Lady's Bedstraw and also hybridises with it. All bedstraws have square stems and flower parts in fours.

Goosegrass, Cleavers
(*Galium aparine*)   **d'l'herbe a tchilieuvre**

Another member of the bedstraw family. Goosegrass is also known as Cleavers or Sticky Willie because the

whole plant is covered with hooked hairs which catch onto passers-by and so is carried to new areas. Children love secretly sticking pieces to the backs of their friends! In the past it was chopped up and fed to goslings. The roasted seeds have been used as a coffee substitute. The young leaves taste like pea shoots and can be eaten either raw or cooked. Applied externally, Goosegrass can ease wounds and ulcers and if eaten it is supposed to relieve cystitis.

Pellitory-of-the-wall
(*Parietaria judaica*) d'l'apathitouaithe
This is a relative of the Stinging Nettle, although it doesn't sting. It is very common in Jersey, growing out of walls and

is quite a pest in gardens. The plants can be male, female or hermaphrodite, with the female flowers growing above the male flowers. If you touch the plant when the stamens are ripe, they will release a cloud of pollen. In the past it

was used to treat kidney and bladder stones as the plant appeared to break the stones of the walls it grew on.

Ivy-leaved Toadflax
(*Cymbalaria muralis*)
Another wall-growing plant with very pretty, tiny flowers. These are lilac and yellow

and resemble a miniature Snapdragon. The seeds have an ingenious dispersal mechanism. The stem with the seeds grows towards the dark, so ensuring that they will be deposited in a suitable crevice in the wall. Ivy-leaved Toadflax was originally introduced from the Mediterranean as a garden plant in the 17th century.

English Stonecrop
(*Sedum anglicum*) **du pain a crapaud**

This succulent plant is common on dry banks. It has white flowers and its leaves are red-tinged. Two other stonecrops are common in Jersey. The Biting Stonecrop (*Sedum acre*) tends to grow near the sea. It has yellow flowers and its leaves have a peppery taste. Another name for it is Welcome Home Husband Though Never So Drunk! The White Stonecrop (*Sedum album*) grows along the tops of drystone walls. It is not native but is naturalised and common.

Black Nightshade
(*Solanum nigrum*)　　　　　　　　du verjus au dgiabl'ye

Despite the name, the flowers of Black Nightshade are white! It is the berries which are black. It belongs to the potato family and is poisonous. It is a relative of Deadly Nightshade – one of Britain's most poisonous flowers, although this is not found in Jersey. Deadly Nightshade is also known as Belladonna, meaning beautiful lady, because ladies in past times took it to dilate their pupils and appear more beautiful – a very dangerous practice.

Woody Nightshade, Bittersweet
(*Solanum dulcamara*)
d'l'amierdoux

Closely related to Black Nightshade, Woody Nightshade has pretty purple flowers with a yellow cone of stamens in the centre. The plant scrambles up through other plants. There are various suggestions for the name Bittersweet. Some say the

poisonous berries are sweet with a bitter aftertaste, some say the berries are bitter but become sweet after chewing and others say the green unripe berries are sweet but become bitter when red and ripe. Whatever the truth of the matter, they are very poisonous, so do not try them!

Thorn Apple
(*Datura stramonium*) **du pommyi du dgiabl'ye**
The large, white trumpets develop into spiny round fruits about the size of a conker in its shell. Thorn Apple grows on waste land across the island. Another member of the

potato family it is also poisonous. In the Channel Islands Thorn Apple leaves were dried and smoked like tobacco to cure asthma.

Kangaroo Apple
(*Solanum laciniatum*)
This plant comes from Australia as its name suggests. It is found on wasteland and roadsides and seems to be becoming more common. The bright blue summer flowers are followed by egg-shaped fruits. These are green at first, ripening to orange. They are poisonous, although

the aboriginal people of Australia say they are edible after they become pendulous – but I wouldn't recommend trying them!

Lesser Burdock
(*Arctium minus*) de l'ouothelle d'ane

This is a biennial plant, producing a rosette of large leaves the first year followed by a huge flower spike up to 2 metres high in the second year. The flowers are similar to round thistles and are followed by the burrs which give the plant its name. These are covered in hooks which catch on the fur of any passing animals and are carried away, so dispersing the seeds. This plant was the

inspiration for the invention of Velcro. A hiker noticed how the burrs were sticking tightly to his thick woolly hiking socks and so the idea was born.

Annual Mercury
(*Mercurialis annua*)   d'la tetue

A close relative of Dog's Mercury, which is rare in Jersey. Annual Mercury is very common along the roadsides and on waste ground. The male and female flowers occur on different plants and look so different that some people mistake them for separate species. It is poisonous, although boiling removes the poison and it was eaten as a vegetable in Germany.

Quaking Grass
(*Briza maxima*)   des lermes d'Jacob

This pretty grass is common along the roads across the island. It is native to Southern Europe, so is badly affected by harsh winters. The nodding flowers bob in the slightest breeze, hence the name. The green flowers

dry to a light brown and then are often used in flower arrangements. They look pretty growing in garden borders but be careful to pick them before they seed or they will take over your garden!

Hare's Tail
(*Lagurus ovatus*)　　　　　　　　**des babinnes-de-lievre**

This grass is used on the floats in the famous Battle of Flowers. The soft seedheads are dyed and made into elaborate patterns and scenes to decorate the floats. Nowadays most of the floats buy their Hare's Tails from Holland, already dyed in a rainbow of colours. Originally from the Mediterranean, you will find it growing mainly along the coast. The Hare's-foot Clover (*Trifolium arvense*) is superficially similar with its woolly flower heads but has the typical trefoil clover leaf. It is common in sandy areas near the coast.

Marram Grass
(*Ammophila arenaria*)　　　　　　　　**du melgreu**

This grass is well adapted to grow in the harsh coastal regions. Its leaves are rolled into a tube so that the underside is protected from the drying sea winds. They also have a thick waxy coating to help prevent moisture loss, which gives the leaves their blue-green appearance. The roots are very long in order to find the little moisture that exists in the sand. However, Marram Grass is also the reason that the sand dunes exist. The leaves trap blown sand and so it grows into a mound. The growing tips of the Marram are stimulated by being covered by sand and grow up through the new layer of sand. This process is repeated and so the sand dunes grow, held together by the extensive Marram roots. However, it becomes a victim of its own success – as the sand dunes become more stable they are invaded by other plants and become less suitable for the Marram Grass. This is called succession.

Sea Beet
(*Beta vulgaris*) **des bettes**

This is the wild relative of beetroot, although it lacks the swollen stem base. It is common around the coast and is also found inland due to seaweed being spread on fields as a fertiliser. The leaves are leathery to reduce water loss, so allowing it to survive in the harsh coastal conditions. In Jersey the leaves were eaten and cooked like spinach.

Yellow Horned Poppy
(*Glaucium flavum*)   des jeunes pavots

This yellow poppy is found in St Ouen's Bay near the sea wall. The name comes from the long narrow seed capsule which can be up to 30 cm long. This splits almost to the base to release the seeds. The stems and leaves are bluish-grey due to being covered in a layer of wax which helps to prevent moisture loss in this extreme habitat. The orange sap is foul-smelling. All parts of the plant are poisonous, including the seeds.

Sea Holly
(*Eryngium maritimum*)   du housse de mielle

Despite its name and appearance this is not a holly or a thistle – it is in fact a member of the umbellifer family. It grows on the sand dunes in St Ouen's Bay, its grey-blue leaves being adapted to conserve water in these harsh conditions. In the past its roots were eaten as a vegetable

and it was also used medicinally. The candied roots were called Eryngo and sold as a delicacy which was supposed to have aphrodisiac qualities!

Tamarisk
(*Tamarix gallica*)
du tamathin

Although it survives well here, it does not produce seedlings, so all the bushes you see have been planted. The leaves are small and scale-like as befits a coastal plant, giving the stems a feathery appearance. The pink flowers grow in spikes at the end of the stems. It can take salt up from the groundwater and exude it through its leaves, giving them a sparkly appearance.

Argentum
(*Atriplex halimus*) d'l'argentinne

The silver-grey leaves give this plant its name, although it is also known as Shrubby Orache. It is used for hedging

near the coast as its leaves are tolerant of salt spray. It produces flowers and seeds, but these don't develop into seedlings here, so it spreads by layering. It was well established in Jersey by the 19th century. It is very drought resistant, being a native of the Sahara desert.

Tree Lupin
(*Lupinus arboreus*) d'l'arbre a lupins

A North American species from California, the Tree Lupin flourishes on the dunes at St Ouen's Bay, growing up to 2 m. The pea-like flowers are yellow and grow in spikes. They are scented and attract many bees and butterflies. A perennial, it is a useful stabilising plant on the sand dunes but can seed rapidly and crowd out other species.

Restharrow
(*Ononis repens*) du ricolisse en bouais

This plant gets its name from its long tough roots which in the past would hold up or 'rest' a hand-held harrow. It has pretty pink, pea-like flowers which attract bees with their scent, although it doesn't have nectar to reward them with. The flowers appear from June to September. The plants may sometimes have soft spines. They are common on sandy

areas of the coast. The roots used to be eaten like liquorice. It was thought that if cows ate the plant their milk would be tainted.

Common Centaury
(*Centaurium erythraea*)
d'l'herbe d'St Martin
This pretty little plant grows in dry areas on the heathlands and sand dunes, often on poor soils. Its pink flowers are stalkless and grow in clusters. It is a member of the Gentian family. Herbalists said it was useful for wounds, and the name is said to come from Chiron the centaur who used it to cure his wounds after being bitten by the many-headed monster, the Hydra.

Sea Kale
(*Crambe maritima*)
du chou-mathin
Easily recognised by its silver-grey, cabbage-like leaves and large clusters of white flowers, Sea Kale can be found growing on shingle beaches. Many parts of the plant, including the roots,

leaves and stems, have been used as food from early times. The Romans preserved it in barrels for sea voyages as it is high in vitamin C and prevented scurvy. *Crambe* comes from the Greek for cabbage.

Jersey Thrift
(*Armeria arenaria*)
d's iliets d'mielle

Both the Jersey and the Common Thrift grow in Jersey, turning the roadside at St Ouen's Bay pink. The Common Thrift flowers in May and the Jersey Thrift later, in late July and August. The Jersey Thrift is also distinguished by its taller flowering stems. It is originally from central and southern Europe and is not found in the other Channel Islands or Britain. Thrift plants are adapted to the dry seaside conditions by having a cushion of narrow leaves and very long

roots which reach down to find water. Because of these adaptations, Thrift can also grow on mountains.

Alderney Sea Lavender
(*Limonium normannicum*)

This little Sea Lavender grows in the middle of St Ouen's Bay, near the White House. It is unscented. As the name suggests, it also grows in Alderney, although it is rare

there, and on the French coast. It is not found in the other Channel Islands. It is thought that it arrived in Jersey during the Occupation on the boots of the German soldiers.

Rock Samphire
(*Crithmum maritimum*)
d'la perche-pierre

This umbellifer is common on rocks around the coast. The thick, fleshy leaves retain water and are an adaptation to living in the harsh coastal conditions. In the past they were collected and eaten as a vegetable, either cooked like asparagus or pickled in vinegar.

The name samphire is a corruption of Saint Pierre, St Peter, who is the patron saint of fishermen and whose name also means 'rock', an apt saint for this plant. The greenish flowers grow in umbels and are much visited by insects for their nectar.

Thyme
(*Thymus polytrichus*)
d'la serpiliethe

Purple carpets of wild Thyme grow along St Ouen's Bay and it is also common on the dunes and heaths. The flowers have a sweet scent and attract bees which are rewarded by nectar for their visit. The leaves are aromatic because they contain an oil, thymol, and are much used as a cooking herb.

Sea Radish
(*Raphanus raphanistrum*) **du breha**

Many yellow cruciferous plants grow along Jersey's roadsides, but one of the commonest is Sea Radish, which despite its name can be found far inland. The yellow, occasionally white, flowers are followed by a seedpod which looks like a row of green beads, ripening one by one.

Rough Star Thistle
(*Centaurea aspera*)
This pink flower is a speciality of the Channel Islands and is common in St Ouen's Bay, although not found elsewhere in Jersey. It has been naturalised on the dunes since 1839. It is related to the Knapweeds and is at the northern edge of its range.

Carline Thistle
(*Carlina vulgaris*)
This is a biennial thistle which grows on the sand dunes at St Ouen and hillsides around the coast. It has straw-coloured bracts which look like petals. These dry on the plant and survive through the winter. The name is a corruption of Charlemagne, the 8th-century Frankish king who was reputed to have used it to cure his army of the plague.

Hottentot Fig
(*Carpobrotus edulis*)
This plant is a native of South Africa where its fleshy fruit is eaten. Its flowers are large, up to 15 cm across and are yellow, turning pink as they go over so that both colours

are seen on the same plant. Its succulent leaves allow it to colonise the cliff faces where there is little moisture and the sun can be baking hot. However, it has become a pest as it smothers all other vegetation and kills the native flora. Simply killing it is no good as its dead stems prevent recolonisation by native species, hence, local conservation groups organise 'Hottentot fig-bashing days' where their members physically pull up the plant from any accessible areas.

Mallow
(*Malva* and *Lavatera*)   eune mauve (Tree Mallow)

Several Mallow species are common in Jersey. The largest is the biennial Tree Mallow (*Malva arborea*). It was often

grown in cottage gardens near the outside privy where its large soft leaves proved very useful! The leaves of the Common Mallow were used as poultices and to treat inflammation. Mallow fruits are a ring of nutlets inside the calyx which children used to call 'cheeses' and played with them.

Salsify
(*Tragopogon porrifolius*)

This is a garden escape related to the British native flower Jack-Go-To-Bed-At-Noon. As the name suggests, the yellow flowers only open in the morning and the purple flowers of Salsify are the same. In the past Salsify was grown as a vegetable. The flowers resemble purple Dandelion flowers and are followed by huge 'dandelion clocks'. The leaves are long and narrow and can easily be mistaken for a grass when there are no flowers.

Teasel
(*Dipsacus fullonum*) **du tcheurdron a chorchi**
This tall plant gets its name from the seedheads which were once used to tease cloth. The flowering pattern is unusual – first a ring of lavender-coloured flowers open in

the centre of the flower head and the flowers then open upwards and downwards from this. The leaves are paired, joined around the prickly stem. Water collects in these leaf bases. Ladies used to use this water to wash their faces to remove blemishes, hence the old name of Venus's Bath. It is a biennial plant, only producing a rosette of leaves in the first year. The seedheads dry naturally and are often used in flower arrangements.

Scarlet Pimpernel
(*Anagallis arvensis*) **la baronmette es pouorres gens**
Also known as Poor Man's Weatherglass from its habit of the flowers closing before bad weather. The flowers are one of the few red native flowers. Pale-coloured variants occur, and white or blue flowers are occasionally seen. The seedpod is a spherical capsule which splits open, the top half falling off to allow the seeds to disperse. It was once valued as a cure for madness and depression.

Bell Heather
(*Erica cinerea*)   **d'la bruethe**

The flowers of Bell Heather turn the heaths purple from late summer through to autumn. It prefers dry areas. The tiny leaves grow in whorls of three and are adapted to conserve moisture in the dry and windy heathland habitat.

Ling
(*Calluna vulgaris*)
d'la bruethe

This heather has smaller paler flowers than the previous species. It is common on cliffs and coastal heaths. Plants with white flowers are sometimes found, the 'lucky' white heather. In the past it was used for fuel, and the name comes from the Anglo-Saxon 'lig' meaning fire. The twiggy stems were also used for bedding and thatching, and made into brooms. *Calluna* comes from the Greek for brush. Bees love heather and make the nectar into a dark, strong-flavoured honey.

Ragwort
(*Senecio jacobaea*) d's entaillies

This yellow-flowered composite grows on the heaths, fields and wasteland. It is very poisonous and is an injurious weed under Jersey Law which has to be controlled – landowners are required by law to remove it. Horses and cattle will avoid it when it is growing in their fields, but they will eat it if it is present in their hay which makes it an especially dangerous weed. However, the caterpillars of the Cinnabar Moth can eat it with impunity, absorbing  the poison and becoming poisonous themselves! They advertise the fact that they are poisonous by their colouring of black and orange stripes – nature's warning colours – which should put off any potential predators. Ragwort grows as a biennial or sometimes as a perennial. *Senecio* means 'old man', referring to the grey fluffy seedheads. Witches were believed to turn Ragwort into a horse so that they could fly across the skies at night. The *Jacobaea* refers to St James, the patron saint of horses, and chemicals from the plant have been used in veterinary medicine.

Great Mullein
(*Verbascum thapsus*) d'la molene

This biennial plant is also known as Aaron's Rod because of the huge flowering spike which can be 1.8 metres (6 feet) tall. The flowers are primrose yellow, the lowest ones in the spike opening first. The leaves forming a rosette at

ground level are huge and downy. In the past they were used as wicks and poultices. During the German Occupation from 1940-45, they were dried and used as tobacco. The Romans extracted a yellow dye from the petals.

Spear Thistle
(*Cirsium vulgare*)   **des soudards**

This is possibly the thistle of the Scottish emblem and has the typical thistle flower with a rounded base and purple florets. These are followed by the thistledown which floats on the wind to disperse the seeds. Children call these fairies or witches and catch them as they float past, making a wish before releasing them. The leaves are very sharp and prickly, living up to its name! It is a biennial so doesn't become too much of a pest, unlike the perennial Creeping Thistle (*Cirsium arvense*) which is also common here.

Tormentil
(*Potentilla erecta*)
d'l'herbe a paralysie

The pretty little yellow flowers of this plant have four petals. The leaves are usually three-lobed. It is common in grasslands and on the cliffs. The name refers to pain or torment because it was used to relieve pain, particularly toothache – the Latin name indicating that it was a potent medicine. It is related to the Cinquefoils which have five petals.

Great Willowherb
(*Epilobium hirsutum*)

Another name for this is Codlins and Cream, codlin being a kind of apple. Bees love this plant as it produces copious amounts of nectar. It is related to the Rosebay Willowherb which also grows in Jersey but is much less common than in the UK.

Herb Robert
(*Geranium robertianum*) **du rouoget**

The origin of the name is unknown – it may be from *rubra*, the Latin for red, referring to the colour of its stems and leaves. Other suggestions link it to Robin Goodfellow, Robin Hood or Abbot Robert, a French Cistercian monk. It also has many other names. The crushed leaves can be used as an insect repellent. It has also been used since early times for grazes and bruises and was held in high repute in the Middle Ages. Little Robin (*Geranium purpureum*) is a similar species with smaller flowers.

Gallant Soldier
(*Galinsoga parviflora*)

Despite the name, this plant is small and weedy, and is a pest in its native America. The name is a corruption of the Latin name *Galinsoga*. Two species occur in Jersey – Gallant Soldier and Shaggy Soldier, which is very similar but has hairy stems and leaves. It seems to be increasing in Jersey, and some cornfields are full of it. It also grows by the side of roads.

Green Alkanet
(*Pentaglottis sempervirens*)

The name comes from 'Al-henna' because of the red dye which can be obtained from its roots. Despite the Green in the name and the red dye, the flowers are actually a striking blue with a white 'eye' – perhaps the bluest of all blue wild flowers. They resemble large Forget-me-nots, to which they are related. The Latin name *Pentaglottis* means 'five tongues' and refers to the five scales at the centre of the flower. Alkanet is common in hedgerows and on roadsides from early summer onwards. It was probably introduced into Britain by monks who used the red dye to colour inferior wines. The green shoots can be cooked and eaten like spinach.

Ramping Fumitory
(*Fumaria muralis*)   d'la finneterre

The name Fumitory comes from the Latin, meaning 'smoke of the earth'. This could refer to the finely divided

grey-green leaves or the spikes of dusty pink flowers, each with around twelve flowers. It is an annual which is common around the island on roadsides.

Sheep's Bit Scabious
(*Jasione montana*)   **des flieurs au dgiabl'ye**

This lovely little plant with its bright blue flowers is not actually a scabious at all; it belongs to the family Campanulaceae and is related to Bellflowers. It is the only member of this family to grow wild in Jersey, although another Bellflower is often seen growing on walls. Another name for it is Blue Buttons. It grows on dry heaths and roadsides. The name may refer to sheep eating it or it may be due to confusion with the similar looking but unrelated Devil's Bit Scabious.

Heath Milkwort
(*Polygala serpyllifolia*)   **d'la stchinnancie**

The Latin name *Polygala* translates as 'much milk' and it was supposed to increase the milk yield of cattle and later came to be used for nursing mothers. The flower is unusual because two of the sepals are enlarged and

protect the rest of the flower. It is these sepals that are coloured. Heath Milkwort is the commonest Jersey Milkwort and is common on the heaths, cliffs and dunes.

Water Mint
(*Mentha aquatica*)   d'la menthe sauvage

This plant is common in wet places and is easily recognised by the smell of its leaves and the ball of lilac flowers at the top of the stem. Although the flavour is not as strong as Garden Mint, the leaves and flowers can be used in salads. In Elizabethan times, mint was one of the strewing herbs used to cover the floors.

Autumn Ladies' Tresses
(*Spiranthes spiralis*)
This orchid is small and easily overlooked in the turf in which it grows. The white flowers grow in a spiral round the flowering stem and so resemble a lady's ringlet or braid. They smell of almonds. The plant can take up to 15 years to flower, so it requires established turf where it won't be overly disturbed – hence it is often found in old graveyards. The plant in the photograph was growing in a lawn with hundreds of others.

Blackberry, Bramble
(*Rubus fruticosus*)   **eune ronche, des mouaithes**
One of the most variable of British plants, over 2,000 microspecies of Bramble have been described and the number is increasing all the time. The microspecies vary in small details of all parts of the plant such as flower colour, leaf shape, thorniness and even taste. So if you

find a patch of Brambles with particularly sweet berries it is probably due to its genes rather than it growing in a good sunny spot. Why not go back the next year and see if the taste is as good? Folklore states that the berries shouldn't be eaten after Michaelmas Day, 29th September, as the Devil spits on them then. The berries do become mushy in late autumn, but it is due to flies spitting on them to convert them to a liquid which they can suck up, rather than the work of the Devil. An infusion of the leaves eases a sore throat when either drunk or gargled. The leaves are often mined by tiny moth caterpillars which leave a white rambling trail across the leaves.

Ivy
(*Hedera hibernica*)

One of the last plants to flower, so it is very important for bees and wasps; a flowering bush will be literally humming with them. The balls of green flowers are followed by clusters of black berries which are enjoyed by the birds. Ivy is a climber and is unusual because its leaves change shape as it gets higher. Those near the ground have five pointed lobes, whereas those growing higher up are simple and look as though they come from a

completely different plant. This is sometimes called Tree Ivy. It does no harm to the trees it grows on as it only uses them for support, although the weight of ivy high in a tree may make it top-heavy and susceptible to high winds. Ivy has been traditionally used as a Christmas decoration for centuries and features in the Christmas hymn, *The Holly and the Ivy*.

The ivy which grows in Jersey is a different species from the Common Ivy found in the UK, although it looks very similar and until recently was considered the same species.

German Ivy
(*Delairea odorata*)

The leaves of this climber resemble ivy, although it is no relation. It is in fact related to Ragwort as can be seen when its small, yellow flowers appear in November – it used to be placed in the *Senecio* genus along with Ragwort. It grows on the Railway Walk near St Aubin amongst other places.

Bibliography and Further Reading

Andrews, J. (1995) *Creating a Wild Flower Garden*, Claremont books

Breverton, T. (2011) *Breverton's Complete Herbal*, Quercus

Keble Martin, W. (1982) *The new Concise British Flora*, Bloomsbury Books

Le Sueur, F. (1976) A *Natural History of Jersey*, Phillimore

Le Sueur, F. (1986) *Flora of Jersey*, Societe Jersiaise

Perring,F., Walters, M. and Gagg, A. (1994) *The Macmillan Field Guide to British Wildflowers*, Grange Books

Press, J.R., Sutton, D. A. and Tebbs, B.M. (1981) *Field Guide to the Wild Flowers of Britain*, Reader's Digest

Sterry,P. (2006) *Collins Complete Guide to British Wild Flowers*, Collins

Streeter, D. and Richardson, R. (1982) *Discovering Hedgerows*, BBC

Index of Common Names

Alexanders 33
Alkanet, Green 87
Argentum 72,
Avens, Wood 45
Bartsia, Yellow 40
Bedstraw, Hedge,
Bedstraw, Lady's 61, 62
Beet, Sea 70
Bindweed, Field 53
Bindweed, Hedge 52, 53
Bindweed, Sea 53
Bittersweet 65
Blackberry 90
Blackthorn 18, 19
Bluebell 13, 14, 15, 23, 31, 32
Bramble, 90, 91
Broom 18
Broom, Prostrate 18
Burdock, Lesser 67
Butcher's Broom 32
Campion, Bladder 31
Campion, Red 14, 30, 38
Campion, Sea 30
Campion, White 26, 30
Carrot, Wild 34, 35
Catchfly, Nottingham 38
Celandine, Greater 24, 45
Celandine, Lesser 15, 23, 24, 45
Centaury, Common 74
Chickweed 26

Cleavers 62
Clematis 47
Cudweed, Cape 10, 58
Daffodil 14, 20, 21
Dodder 54
Elder 46, 47
Evening Primrose 37
Fennel 49, 50
Foxglove 48
Figwort, Balm-Leaved 51, 52
Flag, Yellow 40, 43
Fleabane, Common 58
Fleabane, Canadian 10, 58
Fleabane, Mexican 10, 57
Fumitory, Ramping 87
Gallant Soldier 86
Gladdon 44
Gladiolus, Wild 39
Goosegrass 62, 63
Gorse 17, 18, 54
Green-winged Orchid 42
Hare's-foot Clover 69
Hare's Tail 69
Hawthorn 19, 20
Heather 82
Heather, Bell 82
Heliotrope, Winter 21
Herb Bennet 45
Herb Robert 86
Holly, Sea 71
Hogweed 34

Honeysuckle 15, 47
Hottentot Fig 10, 13, 78, 79
Iris, Stinking 44
Iris, Yellow 43
Italian Lords and Ladies 28
Ivy 91, 92
Ivy, German 92
Kangaroo Apple 66
Kale, Sea 74
Ladies' Tresses, Autumn 90
Leek, Three-cornered 23
Ling 82
Little Robin 86
Loosestrife, Purple 40, 41
Lords and Ladies 10, 15, 27, 28
Mallow, Tree and Common 79, 80
Marigold, Corn 55
Marram Grass 69, 70
May 19, 20
Melilot 51
Mercury, Annual 68
Mercury, Dog's 12, 68
Milkwort, Heath 88, 89
Mint, Water 89
Mugwort 60, 61
Mullein, Great 83
Navelwort 44
Nettle 63
Nightshade, Black 65

Nightshade, Deadly 65
Nightshade, Enchanter's 29
Nightshade, Woody 65
Nipplewort 52
Old Man's Beard 47
Orchid, Autumn Ladies' Tresses 90
Orchid, Common Spotted 40
Orchid, Early Purple 42
Orchid, Green-winged 42
Orchid, Heath Spotted 40
Orchid, Jersey 39, 40
Orchid, Pyramidal 40, 41
Orchid, Southern Marsh 40
Ox-eye Daisy 57
Oxalis, Pink 28, 29
Pellitory-of-the-wall 63
Pennywort 44
Pimpernel, Scarlet 81
Pineappleweed 56
Plantain, Buck's-horn 60
Poppy 55
Poppy, Yellow Horned 71
Primrose 13, 14, 15, 25, 26
Quaking Grass 68
Radish, Sea 77
Ragged Robin 38, 40
Ragwort 83, 93
Restharrow 73
Roast Beef Plant 44
Rose, Burnet 36

Rose, Dog 35
Rose, Spotted Rock 36
Rough Star Thistle 78
Sage, Wood 49
Salsify 80
Samphire, Rock 76
Scentless Mayweed 56
Sea Lavender, Alderney 75
Sedge, Pendulous 42
Sheep's Bit Scabious 88
Shrubby Orache 72
Sloe 18, 19
Snowdrop 14, 22, 23
Snowflake, Summer 22
Soldier, Gallant 86
Soldier, Shaggy 86
Speedwell, Germander 60
Spring Beauty 27
Stinking Iris 44
Stonecrop, Biting, English and White 64
Stitchwort, Greater 26
Tamarisk 72
Teasel 80

Thistle, Carline 78
Thistle, Creeping 84
Thistle, Rough Star 78
Thistle, Spear 84
Thorn Apple 66
Thrift, Common and Jersey 75
Thyme 77
Toadflax, Ivy-leaved 63, 64
Tormentil 85
Traveller's Joy 47
Tree Lupin 73
Valerian, Red 50
Vetch, Tufted 50
Violet, Common Dog 24
Violet, Sweet 25
Western Gorse 17
Willowherb, Great 85
Willowherb, Rosebay 85
Winter Heliotrope 21
Wood Sorrel 12, 29
Yarrow 59
Yellow Flag 40, 43
Yellow Horned Poppy 71

Notes

Notes

Brambleby Books

Other Nature Books by Brambleby Books

Norfolk Wildlife – A Calendar and Site Guide
Adrian M. Riley
ISBN 978 1908241 047

British and Irish Butterflies - The complete Field, Identification and Site Guide to the Species, Subspecies and Forms
Adrian M. Riley
ISBN 978 0955392 801

Birds Words – Poetic images of wild birds
Hugh D. Loxdale
ISBN 978 0954334 734

Arrivals and Rivals – A duel for the winning bird
Adrian M. Riley
ISBN 978 0954334 796

Garden Photo Shoot – A Photographer's Yearbook of Garden Wildlife
John Thurlbourn
ISBN 978 0955392 832

Winging it – Birding for Low-flyers
Andrew Fallan
ISBN 978 0955392 856

Never a dull Moment – A naturalist's view of British wildlife
Ross Gardner
ISBN 978 0955392 870

Buzzing! Discover the poetry in garden minibeasts
Anneliese Emmans Dean
ISBN 978 1908241 078

Birduder 344 – A life list ordinary
Rob Sawyer
ISBN 978 1908241 092

And Listen to the Waves – Selected Poems
Brian Churcher
ISBN 978 1908241 191

Making Garden Meadows – How to create a natural haven for wildlife
Jenny Steel
ISBN 978 1908241 221

Sheer Cliffs and Shearwaters – A Skomer Island Journal
Richard Kipling
ISBN 978 1908241 214